birds carve glass

Jodde Maree

Jodde Maree

Original title
birds carve glass

Cover design
Sonja Smolec

Layout and edit
Sonja Smolec
Yossi Faybish

Published by
Aquillrelle

ISBN 978-1-67818-318-9

vanishing heartlands now wade upon my dusted eyes...

Jodde Maree

Table of Contents

birds carve glass

Unseen

Take me inside places
You've never been mirrored candles
Dancing pronounced defensive
Unseen
Breaking bones into gravitational blood lines
Incoming wave's oceanic rinds flinching peels
Cobra's selenic smile stolen
Lighthouse stems tip top breaking!
My eyes close into shadowed streets rapid howls
Glorious hearts angels on fire!
Aching steam absorbs lifeless clusters of rain
You're waking horizons!
Opening corridors unwrapping chilling mementos
Flinching wings recite your world fluttering echoes
Dwell into oncoming traffic
Fragile darkness night storm headlights
Run

Who Sings

Who will sing for me?
In between shoulders
Of lights rising
Days begging endless of memoirs
No rhyme
No reason
Causeless seasons redirected
Sonic tunes hearts flee into breaking glass
Bloody blistered beats!
Seas' crackling shivers bondless radios
Its fluidities name sake my pulse racing
Gone

Incoming words

Fast words
Just scenes
Just furies
Balloons frying low
Valliant chains don't sit down
Splurges of soul
Crete paper dismisses
Manifesto religion
Stains of anti-Christ malnutrition
Midnight's peeking rain
Slithering sigh eloping views
Hire car blues!

Conceived

First locket's anesthetized pen
Fleeced pictures swimming in concrete
Minds fried into time
Nothing slides!
Melodic freedom
Black house
Black eyes
Night's seething dreams
Alleyways tales!
Snake vender's spits and spats
Polystyrene flares!
Shadows walk beneath my feet
Paint a version of me into winter I want to freeze
Rice bunnies canter by a circle of hymns
I live under your thorns
You call us human beaten by disgust
Diagnosed rods perched upon thriving orchards of thunder
Myths faking lives!
Ostracized manacles gazing lights
Moth pound stripes!
Gazelles of mystical stereos
Plunge

Parachute

Childhood flood lights
No entry –
Shining smiles persecute angels
Switched on tenderness cradles flinch
Slangs arrogance a swiped crossing!
Duality reaches into stolen traffic
Observed intensity wishful skies
Inhibitions alluring perfume platonic wisdoms
I've crackled inside your eyes!
Interpretations threaded by fine papers
Humanly acquired flames!
Your mind bites off hemispheres
Well trained aliases –
Celestial embryos yank my tail!
Don't lie without pitiful chunks
Immaculate pieces seize weightless sound
Open glazier's letters fading palms of grapes
Wire bound heckles!
Gripping Tudor's open heart surgeries
Exile!

Diving Into Lightning

Breaking ice thunder cracks
Go diving!
Stricken glories death pool reflections
Paris rapids spoken oceanic capitals
Mirrored groundings!
You arrive then disappear
I begging of soul
First words laurel ends
Woven attire written intensely versed
I painted shadows upon your walls
Silk sketch's glass staircases!
Crashing cards swiped by thirsty murmurs
Cyprian flowers I've seen you move inside tides of sand
Causes paraglide into open seasons
Ostracized birds!
Sneeze! Out poems
Yanking cupid's tail
Clouds of foamy demolition
Height!

Blonko Ink

Raven's blonde adieu!
Slithering livers curving up sentimental corners
War whores run in pairs –
Hallelujahs incisors wide blade eyes!
I singed your alibi blonko!
My ink size lyrebird!
Pin sucked pennies rolling on ice
Throw the dice!
Dip strange ways with ink!
Fry on dying horizons!
I'm there! Where?
Here right here!
My minds a blood shot exploding
Did you look at your mirrors of assailing flesh!
Our breeze is ripe
With pocket book songs
Sing to me you bleu flu!

Black Reservoirs

Pitched in space
Nights a bird's haven –
Rinsed out cologne watered down soul!
I'm pinched again!
Skin sounds moan into thin air!
I said rare!
No it's a wild bare!
Leisurely cynics breaking bread!
Black Gods
Water high balloons skimming the edge!
I took a pulse today!
I flipped out of zen –
Slow running water only leaks from taps!
Where's the reservoir Gap's
Where's the flood?
I want bulging prestige!
Waist thick in dark invitations!
Why did you mold my soul?
Aren't we supposed to gravitate on cutting boards!
Light legs won't carry stilts!
You have to jump!
How high?

Figure Skating

Icy words charming mind
How the hours walked on by
Sweat bound hands open fires!
O' figure!
Lights go leaping out of windows!
I'm skating solo –
I heard your voice yesterday!
I saw through your misty call!
Opulent perils scoped my blood!
I'm leading myself into a tub of razors
Is the wire of your skin clean!
Let me bleed you open -
My hairs scattered all over your eyes!
A breezy whisper falling high!
Don't count me as a day
Don't count me as a week
Don't count me at all!
I'm awake not a ewe in your sleep
Dream on little bird!
Now fly away –
I won't turn back as you run away
Just sail upon my perfume while your essence burns

Jumble Rush

Glass birds cut you she said
While puttering heads vividly cream into avenues soaked in juice
Cranberry words slow motion sweeps / So drips our world of inconsequential beliefs
Midday connoisseurs moving along sliding tides / Sipping away high bridge bound lines
Out of sync air cage sunk yesterdays
Blood vein chorus's now inspired into black ink
Cold sliced verse / A parachute flies above your mind
Blue silent tonics tall pier goodbyes
Crocodile jumbles quick break bites!
Slithers of skin derived from your thighs / God's sent parakeet's lyre bird fire
Minutes translated into oncoming hours
Inland burial grounds / Sun brushed with Now
Shaded crash sites Columbus's mourned clouds
Luminous rain / Paradise's prowlers howl
Stair case pulses trauma carved curves
You're alive
Amidst extreme pollinations of extraordinary pearls
Go drink your stained currents split open by your bubble yoke pride
Just feed me somehow / I want to catch lions

Plato's Marrowbone

 ----- blood sealed bursts -----
Wicked splendor microbe gravity / O! Night's relay a screaming hyena
Dark coliseums resin soaked rips / Stars crisp with thunder crash like cement
Marrowbone wire torn applause midnights a sister come whisper late shores
I'm pinched by chaos words are swindlers
Collaborated philosophies plum juiced Plato's
Minutes replace our mercy
I lay right there upon your rails sharp bone horns glared into my light struck eyes
It's a flare Plato's hairs on fire I'm racing against myself
Illicit color's wide spread pilots air buried snares
Icy amuse shattered glass it's all crashing
Glorious scents envisaged verse I'm still running into you
Spinal cord smiles delayed our dune ashes blistered ears O' wake me
Slides of high skies raised on substances of Rembrandt hitching my way to colossus
You raise your hands to air I'm breathing you here!
Lips scented wet by tides my eyes crawl into corners of your extravagance
Did you reach into tomorrow without a word of all you knew?
I called you my antiphrasis standing on your head a white elephant singing
My peril won't touch the ground!
I'm dead inside of you no words to say days are now closed
Did you feel ripe plots justify your cursing blood?
Did you fling yourself out of style?
I rushed into rain just to watch you blow inside immaculate breeze
It was there I watched you fall into carousel thorns / pulled apart by wisdom
Sartre lightning a glimpse of us

Reclusive High Dive

Memento's reining paradise
Macabre ghosts wade upon felt tipped lines
Notes undressed by amnesties of chainless prayers
Internal flinches highly swung birds
Miles choose openly among bled stray pawns
Waters edge's shallow paper's dipped in muse skins
Clouds of pure maneuvers quite fondly perched by inexistence
 I've breathed inside oak stained enemies
Sleek transitions / Translucent scales of ivory blue
Oceanic circus's my words cut from severed chords
Multiplied easels painted with dissolve
Skeptics fluently seize my resolved silence
Sunset's filled with wild groomed pharaohs
Charcoal darned cloth illuminated chills
Blood's ink rich scented extinction
Mindless holly hell imitated soul –`
Celestial pinning a narrow brush wasted
Epigraphs seethe within places I refuse to see
Imaginary rope I felt God's unfiltered eyes
Nights a lying bed of silk –
Heavens reclusive heights dove for me

Elixir

----- glassed out head's shaded blood -----
Verse cubes hit your tongue furiously slashing you're hound heart bled body
Headstone of gravity I'm silence rushed out into the open
My head's a manifested cage iris bird's fly upon waves of destructive wings
My language will die today
Bull ink flies my promissory delays exposed
Where's life's last initials I want to sign into heaven
My elixir of paradise my enviable out spoken slush
It's a bird's mangle a watery hemisphere of clouds
Almighty by space I crawl upon streets of verse
My ordinary longing released into air
My open lines my only human voice now lives in poetic utopia
Dare not return I'll eat you again
Inside anyone don't you know?
It's always high noon
Snaring responses exalts cagy music
Humming straddle tops you've flung into drains
You're high towers peer back at you with elevated delight
Ascended ends you choose to hide
Oblivious rules evaporated eyes you're still blind -
Crumbled fleeces of arrogance persuaded by deluded depth
April fools first day nausea / Dreaded seeds of sparkling ice
Vacancy required

Senso

Contemporary evaporations now summer's yields
Oceanic finch cold sea tonics
Heaven's longing cups of roses
My white sheeted armies my ink stained lips
Saturn's racing heights I stand wide eyed!
I contemplate with God my philosophical annihilations
Illuminated by my inner voice recouped tenderness days lucid of drifting leaves
Imminent edge's insightful echoes
I am air will I survive inside my own eyes
Walk within me placid fires let nothingness caress each unique mood
My Venetian eloquence moving do I appease you?
Words encompass sky lit rooms orchards of living metabolisms of youth
My shelters rain dripping ripe opulence
My imagination of living blooms beautiful miles my scented photographs
Space a palatal playground evaporates without a sound
Am I still vanishing by Delia's grace?
Talkative silence I'm looking at my own human secrecy deficient by entitlement
Mirrors don't reply of darkness my epitaph wonders?
My only skin immersed –
Cradles stillborn memoirs
I senso dream inside poems verse life's lilacs of emptiness
My hallucinogenic gravity
My milky soul
Why do my words unravel without – adieu?

Siren

Raven swiped highlights wing sleek domains
Nights ascending lights split into yielding satellites
Birds pry swing by -
Inland voices icy isolated rush's
Notes captivated in air my dream state velour
Dismantled doll cinema soaked plays O' Hamlet!
My lips slice clouds
Owl lids ink
I won't close my mind
Gravities waves essential blue
Granulated plains celestial zoo
Whose proud wonderland?
Inevitable of ash
Ripe wades illuminate color
Sea bred -
Open spelt seizures silk spun race
Sirens
Circulated circus's cradled apparatus
Cyanic chills
Who?
Esplanades seethe of life's tales
O' how naïve our youthful verse bleeds
We ate innocence out of leaves
Critically absent opulently wise
Ink stained skies too quickly into seasons we dive
Whose love ever dies slowly?
Who?

Birdie

Luminous tweaks
Grey resin eyes alluring clouds perch upon night
Fly away with your fried words
Flutter Flutter....
Lovingly words curl and grate into solemn prayers
Sultry streets blinking of ink stained lights
Kaleidoscope hours come drifting toward your solitude
Silk rain pours upon vanishing reflections
Faint with tepid arousal silhouette roses arise
Dear blood dreaded blood!
My own voice/ I repeal birdie
Inside me I carry fiery stairs to starry nights
My silence a wonderland finch's brutality

Absent

Absent from words
I fall into pools of wondering hours
Absent from herds of voice
Scream scented wild roses running for miles
Candles burn where words cannot be found
I cannot remove places of non-existence only lines
Absent of echoes now stained in ink
I show you my hands I say my hands are strong
In rapids they beat of weightless song
Your words are water encumbering winds of storming rains
Absent of muse yet never neglectful of truth
Infinite landscapes reveal shadows of prowling eyes
I won't be there absent of my own voice
I disappear

Butterfly Sting

Wrapped in black silk bows
My guising words bath in twilight's stillness
Curdling miles
Ink's death print
Reflective verse shredded shadows
Spontaneous voids
Poetic rouge blood line
Soul assassin
Who awakens rain?
Celestial arousal announced by thin air
Ethereal stings
One's mind terminally invaded
A butterfly bee's accountant
Anointed by a dying spring

Playful Rooms

They dream of destiny
Playful rooms awaiting news of Columbus
Places relived by kaleidoscope vision
Impede upon night's darkness
Playfully I've seen
Eyes of starlight's fade
Impeding smiles glazed in depths of shadow
I too swam inside a sea of souls
Effortlessly giving away a part of me
Playfully I've belonged to nothingness
Inescapable paradoxes
Desirable ache a stream of blood and bone
I too bled red skies of roses
I too wept inside palms of seasonal Gods
I too ran beside wild joys of fallen leaves
Playfully

Lockers

You've take a sip yet your lips evaded territorial displays
Once crispy echoes now rumors mourned
Sounds of impressionist do dream cold
Lucid complexions benevolent eyes sensory coupled hands
You gave your head away
Oblivious!
Versatile minds pervaded by reptiles
Absolute grains!
Quintessential youth's unspoken words
Planetary genetics
Make them love you push harder!
Vitalities ruinous quotes
Destroy young hearts steal lead off their tongues
Lockers
Life's unimaginable disguise
Your candy licked skies abode
Stranger's time has betrayed you!
Suburban streets washed clean across charcoal canvases
You'll need doe?
Now forecast the rain
You'll learn how to bake cakes
Vitalities sugar coated membranes
Soak in deep sea tanks
Lockers

Paper At Her Feet

Dark sunshine
Summers dawn absorbed
Horizontal fluids drip into swollen rapid
Bedded earth existential synchronism wire longer than life
I splitter splatter my polluted ink!
Silent echoes release paper at my feet
Lying dying a wild urchin's fool
My eye lids are shells crackling beneath stones of fire
My blood bursts here I am surprised again
Wiggling inside a can of worms
I pop the lid only to find paper at my feet
Seas of bread and honey melt away my own existence
Inside my unchartered red cells aligned lions
Rip flesh from my bones

Chilly

It's a chilly night
Patient skies immerse upon wires
Quitting clouds now declare high flying lines
Parachutes won't dissolve the fall one by one
Ink fed charm affluent silence
I take slices of bread verse baking myself in explosive jackets
Pins enthrall needles it's chilly inside button less courtesy
Popping free pouncing flights on air you've caught a stone in your eye
Shivering kaleidoscopes a cities hangover you're a rye
A season of riddles diced in pure rain
Cut out your paper hands make copies of love
It's chilly as I look inside you!
It's so cold smoothing dreams along your skin
I've torn out glossy stains which bore a resemblance of you
Ashes of water now collide on cider scented miles
It's chilly on choking seas piers raised in wild gaze
I'm flourishing into a closing orchid
White heir of sanity gravities girl -
It's chilly inside your smile

Flock Of Naked Snow

How much lower can my voice be?
Naked of coldness I'm barking in flocks of naked sea
Ash top grain my lips release raptures of sliding snow
Antipathies of exiled openness fleeing in ink
My tongue performs in a palace of disappearance
Midnight's future phenomenon hailed rushes
Misunderstood collisions cryptic scenarios condense my words
I fry on a table of conditions
I paint floral columns of my humane existence
Withdrawn from breakage yet elegantly dissolved
Naked

Photographic Paradise

Don't stop at the lights!
Can darkness arrive any quicker?
I reach into sounds of night
Faces absorbed by reflection
Astute movements arranged disguises
Photogenic paradise doesn't stop!
Defused scenery red blue and green!
Humane functioning retrievable desire
Gravel steeple's build dunes of falling words
Unleashed birds carved out of glass cages
Hours absorbed by rhythmic parallels
Life's threaded chaos parked in middle of a screaming child
Habitorial delays retributions of staining noise
Diced romanticisms left summers breeze upon tips of your hair
Look around take a bite of my words they are airless of men
Conditional truths condensed by loneliness
Yet your feet barely touch the ground!
Don't stop!

Grain Powder

Deluxe confusion my blood rinsed by bone
My heads a kerosene fragment!
A waving bird flying above weight
My ears ring with dying
My own words immersed in deflective silence
Shattered glass breaks into my incidental transfusions
My eccentric ash now falling
I've invented plausible decoys
My eyes dripping of colored signals
Clouds emulated me into high powder
Upon eternal seas my souls an only child
Wading seasons of pinnacle Gold
Immaculate ink memoir lines my existential ego
Proposing to God

Oblivious Blood

Hindsight night's crawling rules
Blood soaked angel's room in a house of sadistic discharge
Charismatic capture serene sounded slurs
Deadly inhibition ground blended worms
Oblivious!
Shadow fork words high heel vampires
Let me suck out your lonely skies!
Body secrets entwined opened gates of hell
Strange love locks!
Your silence serves in sky high deserts
You've picked thorns from your dreams
They call you traders while carousels burn
Scrapping rain from ominous winds
Tie down my tongue words are living death
Whispers scented with silk lining say again!
Breezy configurations air born bouquets
Oblivious!

Meat/Money

Sandwich filled questions
Words walk without feet
Sleeveless honey no sweeter than lemon
You take a page from my dreams piling masquerade scenes on your tongue
Sarcastically meat slides from fragile dollars
Don't ask blindness for days of weather
It's just monetary crystal breakages of chandelier rain
My hairs a strain of rumbling beans
May I squeeze venom from your bones?
You crushed my eyes into powder
There my sooth song crawls upon venetian snow
Stretch out my baked perfume with your hands
Tell me your fate?
I want to walk inside a fire of waving birds
Let me appeal to your silent violence!
Smooth eclectics of our unspoken velour
Sky diving into pieces of unsound planets
Absolutely our openness made waves of brutality
I forgive every essence of your breathing

Sesame Bread

Baked in sesame doe
My minds sly shadow eats me
Awake in slices of granulized culture
I'm a flare coin popping!
Senseless pavements categories of desire await my unlicensed ink
Continuous stairs wind upward my open words hung out to dry
Unappeased tongues mortally spun corridors my heads caught inside a sparrow's lair
My thin line prayers recall fellowship apes taking a territorial stand upon
deadly curves of a city
Ducking weaving falling down unapologetic destitution of sounds
Critical grinds broken capillaries of siren red density scenic polish
My head lies holly scented with exodus wildly infused eternally dying
My plated seeds enriched ply bone poetically seized fragments
Self-imposed exile aluminous stillness my remains of me

Camel Cramps

I lift my skin breaking into dreamland homes
Caught in cathartic ties spring's arrived on mars
My hands are cramps laying infinite layers
Choking on life's carousel congested with esteem my prolonged goodbyes
A veneered rooster collecting charm
City souls leave my mouth splitting blood in transit
I immersed myself in scenic paradoxes a camel's meteorite
Spoke heirs splitting chills upon misty morning
I woke again walking on flexible wisdom
No one is blind?
Deep dark passages friendly avenues of Night
Aerosol strings enthralling crescendos live poisonous high wire attire
Systemic feats screeching squeeze out my marrowbones synchronicity
No one is blind?
Canvases of cramped riddles charcoal induced fumes my minds painted occupied
I'm a human collision born under interchangeable skies

Tulip Transience

Petrified sirens maul screaming pilot lights
White cities a cucumber being peeled by sonic scenes
Highlighted fuel static riddled perfume
Take a chunk of my consciousness
Bridal nest fire escape forbidden planets
I'm alive kicking you away!
I've sunken into poetic seas climbing on a ledge
Transient colors breed nightingale suspensions
Perched ignorance I flew into my own slumber just to pull chords of faithful tulips
Squeezing singular rhythms digging my bones from under ground
Follicle ashes white bread opulence I'm found!
Clever riddles sensuous internments
Wishful dishes bounce off my sink in circus processions
Para line echoes feed windswept lullabies
Fragile complexions torn away with soul
Beat me! / It's a winter's voice yelling at you!
I'll climb upon windows of sleepy poems just to seal a deal with God
What's an apparition of fears?
Deluxe tornados leaving unthreaded stems of listlessness
Changing tides paraded in columns of justice
Why?
Move yourself enough to discover there's an emptiness of doubt
Toothpaste soldiers white shiny smile!
Take a shower in depths of sonnets you dare to hide
Wash away your last breath of consideration
Call a friend!
You're dying in front of my eyes
And days don't mean anything at all
You're too tall!

Pinnacle Motion

Light height gales right there above you
Can you see yourself dancing naked?
A fruit tree of seeds dropping verse
Pitched night's fry on your sleeping lids
Wake up stormy let the stars evaporate your existence
Humans in motion car headlights without reason
Transient supper lifeless I sing too
Put me in a middle row call out my name to Friday
Ill forget names you've seen in magazines
A collar of coated arms a sword string pause
Will you wait up there where I can't see you vanishing anymore?
Pinnacles edged out my mind upon glowing strays of miles
I drove into places of dark falling leaves
The chilling hours keep me at ease I'm falling too!
With sounds of infinite apologies I want!
Did you feel dripping sounds of dying roses fleeing your mouth?
Oh poetic substance I'm cursed by the yielding surfaces of you
Culminating into arrows forever lost inside a musical box
The twisting curves of every gravity
A nose dive chalice a symphonic gore
Around a rounded ease I too insensitively devise
Wild nature's of a cold breathing child!

Plausible Immunity

Clucks of blood stones a forest on fire
Stop swirling inside turntable of youth
Perpetual coliseums yearning territories of disguise
Lyre! Lyre!
Love child's hallucinated worm
Buried in sunken dirt just dirty!
The worlds a plausible excuse you tried to burn
You too have fallen upon avenues lost in sequences of red
Crimson fumes strewn blossoms of lovers of starry night songs
Still yelling! Soundly break a spine try mine!
Opal opportunist running on synchronized fury
You're not immune to pulses of whimsical delusion
Spreading seeds of obvious doubt calling out ferns planted for miles
It's a dead wood palace pulling out capsules of rain
I'm pluck I'm stuffed put me on a mantle of silence
Under guard a translucent page your only self-immerses again
Counted days of human material

Flipped Tuxedoes

White menstrual boroughs sugar plated skies
Apricot spaces oppressions worn by little black ties
Flipped out palladiums de sensitized opulence
Questionable exchanges gather up lip sore words
A Crystal barn of celestial adornments peculiar swallows
Fly! Fly!
Sell me a song about Jesus!
He too once walked on stone!
Quintessential buffalo's hung up on miles preached!
No one's home no one dared!
Watery eyes slippery smiles
Sleepless sounds fueled by weightless tarantula lies
Slow steady lies
Flipped out tuxedos predicted drive ahead
High rise oxygen interns of opulent semesters in Florence
Choke hold gildings configurations of exposure
Humane snaps break a lens bow down!
You are amused amusement. Laugh out loud!
Mirrored walls of crackling' kaleidoscope blindness open your ears stop
listening to yourself
Flip your black bow!

Cloud Pinch

Incisors of inky rain falls
Palettes of sky break open on my handy work
Letters of Paris a week too late everlasting stones built waist high
Umbrellas cover swinging moods with days of remembrance
Powder white inhales calling on snow lit steps
Cloud pinches devastated aspirations color behind your thin lines
Corridors of ghostly exposures rails rapid with picture frame smiles
Hello heaven! I ran again...
Turning turnstiles above tracks of your memory
Aqua marine bubbles! Blow away bubble gum trains
I smoke outside air riddled with silent pilots
Blue jean whispers carried along ash black pathways
Did you walk in wet weather?
I saw apart of you in swallow's dew?
Tiny branches broke there with fragile courtesy
Monkey barking accordions playing tik tak with fiddling violins
Painted textures reside in canvases unspoken of unmovable hours
Stop pinching me!
I want summer in a day!
Jump over my soul I want to dance in soulless retreat!
Quaint pities are cruel don't swim in less than your own skin
You're a breathing candescent blow up like a balloon
Lights envy you at breaking speed
My eyes lids are smashing upon fragrant petals
Rose thorn wave of critique shatter in endless winds
Prepare to be amazed by the colors you design
There's no one else here but a night's current
And dark shadows wept with goodbyes

Play My Silence

It's just a room I buried in contours of myself
I splash around like playful child
Ink substitutes pry on my darkness
Hush! Wanders into your world you picked of rice
It's my silence I'm a volunteer
Don't collaborate with written undertones
I fell into Godly betrayal clouds of rich rain stole my pride!
It's a wet afternoon configurations conspire in deadly dreams
Wooden masks explode into splinters skinning my knees
A blueberry hive made of sea splashing ink
Don't touch anything
Put my brushes and paint in clear membrane jars
Clean your skin of conscious apologies
Don't send empty letters written away with falling birds
Lines of scenic apparitions fly into my shadow of deliverance
I hung etches of candescent sky like curtains
Playing Hannibal's hermit I wrote chaos into verse
A line thin child screaming into air
Don't count me in your blessing I'm not good at believing
My paradoxical entries lie in my own head
I walk on window frames shouting please me!
Flocks of imagery relay eternal sounds
Thunderous strides penetrate meticulous voltage
Incensed by duplicate crashing starry mirrors look into my eyes
I hear steps I once took I walk behind my own head
I see into everything I love
I don't want to hear you again

Gap Slice

Did you freeze in frames of paradise?
Crashing waves replay blue memoirs inside my still eyes
Don't fall there it's cavity of weightless mouths
Don't fight back arms which open gaps!
Why you followed yesterday again beneath low fences of empty miles
Sandstone rocks stared high with your equivalent fever
Changeless sea requires a silence you pretend to ignore
Too young to swallow broken static too alive to leave
Who's harm in dying?
How far did you run with panicked consideration?
You wave from a side of the world no one can find
Swimming with ghosts weightless upon endless breeze
I can hear you laughing strung out on dreams
I peer into your eyes within summers guise are you still there?
I've whispered to wild cliffs with lively sonnet!
No one answers back
Watery shallows replace moving tides in and out washing away sound
Caves of shelved echoes break open and burst inside rooms were you once breathed
Swam out curls nights on high wires!
I thought I heard laughter in the shape of changing winds!
You took a slice out of life then life sliced back!
Inevitable betrayal life's lost courtesy
Youthful balconies of buried lullabies
Weightlessness light headed immersed in blue horizons
More a dreamer than anyone could know
Way too young for fall
Way to beautiful for empty journeys
Gaps of unopened letters melodies sung of torn souls

Sample Prophet

Portable ingestions reflective eyes
I walked along promises of broken glass
Prophets engulf high dives
Baring barons of silhouette theatre
Just a taste ill make kid of you
Hypocrite oaths placid interpretations
Just dance with music forget the choir you're always alone
Allow life's perfume to take a hold of you
Stepping left to right wait till you side step your own mind
Tunnel vision lens sample a make believe carousel
Colorful engravings what's your favorite riddle?
Pull yourself apart put a set of ear phones on
Just play like you play!
Don't throw your wishbone away it's a line I threw at you!
Complicated simplicity can't speak of you
Just don't turn around again!
Naive human skin won't elate your powerless hours
Baby sample voice silky quiet attire
You snarl in decibels of prophets singing clearly of wild sands
Verse perched tonics youthful quotations samples of reply
Don't look for parts of your non-existence
You are poetically sold

Teleport Ash

Silky sea pitched silk borrows my restlessness
My shimmering skin inhales weightless shine
Invisible communication teleport voice
I keep looking outward into night's broken eyes
There's too much space before every in-between
I think of science which answers spells I cannot explain
Open pulse musical parades vein sinking ash
Corridors of a sleeping city heavy upon my clipped lids
Symmetrical bones cook my frying words
Inside a room of reflective colors
Mirror tall memories run into splattered clouds
I look to clues of intoxicated sky asking release me with your whispers to God
My neck pulled straight I place my head on a chopping block
Speak to me about every imaginable contour touch my heart with blissful lullabies
My ears are balloons take me away silent breeze!
My thoughts in love with drifting –
Could I feel any taller rising like a stalk of wild human?
Open my soul with infinite proposals I'm lying upon floral tainted grounds
of your birth
Must we meet without need?
Tides are bound around my feet ashes eaten away with poetic ammunition
I'm fighting with a stranger where am I?
My reality is here dying in fire my own words burning
Internal infernos I carry lines of myself across thresholds
Gathering cloaks of my unmistakable identity

Bondi Harp

Violin textures release waves in combinations of rolling silk
Yet string less voices enhance bright street splashes
Better a bird than a prayer?
Whip lashed scenic pools reverse into reflective carousels
Clashingly cold pathways spill stepping grounds of soul
Faded jeans busted shirts button blue eyes take sips of sea glass beaks
Let's pick-up sticks of stones who are better liars?
Let's dive into impeccable harps of melted slurry fashions
I will smash against those homeless waves leaving poems of captured grace
My shadow peaks over your shoulder curling into your chasing moments
Airless summersaults now wade inside my skin
I'll stare at loves mortality beneath a sensitive starry guise
Do not repeat me I will fly out of you!
Bondi harp you played me!
I want these wishful waters to rise into nothingness!
Faithfully disappearing inside chaotic silence lamented by a warm shepherd's coat
Symphonic extracts come alive as scents of you are released into my hair
Dreamy breezes wondering dissolving into past and present
Our living eternity sung in theatrical flair!
We will fall into harps of dawn crystalized among yesterday's souls
Enlightened precious youthfully bled!
Ink lined airless ages of us alone

Glass Mouth

Abalone shells a mustard sting bee
Let me take water from your weary tongue
I fed myself with quail blue bird horizons
Shattered jaws opulent exposure pouring sequences of rain
My ceilings a glass riddled jar I retreat inside cells of amniotic blood
Exchanging letters of Parisian palaces walking on clouds
My careless lines are teeth stoked in fire
Quills of angels provoke my wisdom
Bridge storm petals rose thorn glares upstairs that way
Choking on my own mouth sinister by name of sister
Berry blanched crusades squeezed sour juiceless grains
Splitting with spatters of circular ink
Let's draw strokes against wind calibrated semesters of putrefied tonics
Where did a soul leave you song less?
Sub typical pavilions Puccini's lyre framed in steal corridors
Watch makers of widow sleeve trains abandoned without subway notes!
I'm punching holes into my own heart!
I truly bled on Mars!
How faraway can you be?

Caligula Skirt

Pinch size birds pull away cord clouds
Skin scenic butterflies inhaling God's handiwork
Suckling rains of acquainted rooms -
Chairs of sea chain link children are bare
Caligula's femininity famished stone prose
Delicate titles delinquency sneezed
Orchards of wildly inhibited white sea snails
My attire of celestial despondence now cleansed of youth
Grape mode strobes lightening's priceless flock
Fabricated clocks have stolen my strung daylight
Interchangeable highway a watery ink bred finale
Cotton popped pictures absorb paint from my eyes
I've made a space inside hours which do not fit me
My hands now tied by poetic fascination
Voices of me spike high
Caligula

Monstrous Amour

Verdi's summersaulting concerto violins of dance clouds
High winds elegantly dazzle thin sliced air
Crisp flints of flaring bulls outrageously snarl
Monstrous love letters written by pulse dangling mutilations
Daring trapeze riddled questions?
You continue ripping hearts into paper clip coats
Translucent powder inked in winters made of camouflage expiry dates
Seedlings rise under a snapping sun don't speak a word
Fermented lines formulated by turning symphonies
Whistling sonnets of amour artificial gravity choirs pleated in rows
Intoxicated by toxins blooms ingest substances of effortless essence
Oceanic tides seized by silence selling perfumed apparitions to lonely skies
Rustic voices of sandstone vultures resist wordless worlds of dust
I stood in opposition of soulless Vikings
Yet wades of ocean peer upon my tumultuous vigilance
My hands are human apricots plentitudes of crystal flowers
Versing ghostly memoirs heartlands fueled by entertaining Gods!
Monstrous amour how tall you envision yourself
Rummaging through veins of boneless children your own compositions smile
You are there thriving inside each capsulated mile alive
Eclectic insertions peeled away by pecking orders of photogenic film
Assailing inside you until there's nowhere left to go
You cannot build within holly rooms molding sacred shadows upon walls
Mirror fueled balloons painted with stray strokes of utopia
Monstrous amour you ply me with ink
I dance upon your grave childishly yelling
I'm dying of you

Split Rain

Morning letters of blue silky seas arrive again
Cities lights perish with dawns evaporating haze
Anonymous light splits into poetic visions of silent pause
Spilt rain drips into armless avenues of abandoned sound
Shadowy contours evaporate upon vanishing staircases
My motionless world now abides beneath rising seas
Faint charcoal sketches dipped in artificial realms of living
Collectable streets rinsed clean with linguistic palmistry
Gravity wants to paint me boneless
Interrogational technics closing blind eyes
Cleansing seas ingest apparitions of drifting glass
So smoothly wading depths sooth my soul
Chestnut eyes exhale views of eternal love
Spilt rain releases air into waterless colors
Sandstone houses speak stoically of remaining yesterdays
Endless sea breezes hold weightless birds tinged in rustic freedoms
I know beauty truly
I thrive inside your eloquent cascade
I shall dream of you again split rain my quiet lonely town

Dying Empire

Embers of translucent elegance fade
Steps mold into broken pathways
I hear crackling inside fires side rooms breaking into split flares
I don't want to stretch away strangers I've become
A vision of vanishing flowers I steal my own reflection?
I refuse to be grounded by silence humming inside your mind
Statically versed air reluctantly dresses in embers
Which part of my mirroring exposure actually seized empires?
Thick stains of blood line ink substitute's immovable petrified bodies
Standing doorways of my eyes catch glimmering hints of fatalistic skies
Scratching motion out of minutes requiring rhythms fleeced by oncoming trains
Lively dying ignited here vain strobes wombs of reuniting
Fragile seeds ascend my consciousness just like rain
They land upon peering voices of worldly rituals
I may just be a tin lovingly noted finale a letter to God!
I continue in designs outstretched by landscapes compiling immaculate mercy
I've written myself away into soundless intrigue
Stepping in and out of sacred childishness
Birds carve glass in midst of midnights abyss quietly luring stony words
Un-punishable excuses hours fallen elocution grounds
Birds' reply within faint shadow rising out of gaps left by abandoned -------
Correlating seas built upon symphonies of appraised humane correspondence
Intermediate interpretations symbolic brushed stroked ash
Accumulated choirs listlessly return days back to they're originality
Quintessential longing accented paternity
Where does one truly belong?
I wear my own sacrificial blaze of knowledge
I continue into accelerated burning
Releasing incumbencies of mortality
No one can call me there

Sensuous Evaporation

Pitches of black ovals darkness a fond frolicking pigs tale
Scenic neon's collaborate against nights bustling sky
U-turns of poetic street verbs brighter than glowing stars
Cars meddle in white middle roads plush balconies of head strung eyes
You wear soul like a pin stripe suit accordingly accountable
Sensuous evaporations emptied of overcrowded minds
Thick silk ribbons tie stories of unspoken color
Aquatic premonitions wade inside arms of God!
Melodic renaissances bark at dawn's infancy
Suckling apricot skin bled anti clock wise
Interchange parallels stare down from stilts of idleness
I'm stepping on your abyss!
How high can you jump!
Continuous love lye's on soaking grounds
I see myself inside quiet shadows I too stare at my own outline
Murdering etches of claustrophobic reflection
Digging into isles of Rome held up with paper thin air
Anticipated awakenings my dreamful rainy season
Voiceless stereos roam in corners of past lives
Glass house bodies don't shoot me as prey?
You'll speak down worldly rules!
Human sacrifices calling Jesus a fraud!
Swan Lake was not contrived by a mental ghetto
Dancing off walls plagiarizing milky confections
Spilling dust bean yards all over town ignorantly willing
Chaotic promenades slide into white seconds my words only?

Bus Trade Wire

Faces of steam look left to right you gave in again?
Necks stroked in olive branches glare out torn windows color faintly disappears
Chairs of buoyancy bobbing in dreams of emotional futility
Etched out names aligned with pretentious gloss
You want to change a record by turning heads
Wire fumed outlines trade love for mercy
Terminal sounds relayed with predictions of heavens foundation
Childish mesh cloth roundabouts championship sparrows
You pull your hair from wind shields of freedom
Semesters of youth travelling wild!
Broad stroke sunset's too bright to see?
Thick glassy eyes thick grass fed words
Opinionated Neapolitans linguistic funerals
Let's ride on fragrances of intestines splitting white yarns
Balls of wool bound in pictures of forgotten natures
You think you saw journeys yet you only caught tales
Transcendental blows end in paws of dark illusions
Empathetic pawns rehearse spiritual versatility
Immediate fluidity falls written upon dirty floors
Humane accusations a remaining fool's lair
Souls are ascending behind a season of clouds
Blood transfusions voice to voice!
I am real can you pick me off?
Peel my pockets with life's empty hours
I'm travelling with pick pockets they steal skin from my mouth
My note book of remembrance I sat inside black stained crowds
Stamp trade bus lines free fall snares
Wire!

Butter Wine

It's upon our sincere bread flickering red
Stainless steel teeth biting sound
What's eating you?
Smooth flora's thick butter the endless exaggerations
Live worms bullets of glory simple extracts drunk on wine
Youthful voice! A child's toy jittering poetic fuel
I'm drawing lines on your skin it's warm beside insanity
Nights luster a peeling tongue my angel reborn!
I'll find you in hell beneath precious lifeless hours don't go away!
I'll send you roses while preaching to God cheating on your worlds of love!
Man /woman/child alive with sounds of rivers your pulse my pulse our death!
We fragments of our desirable eternity did feel mickey's mouse compassion
Synthetic floors wear heavenly shoes glass chrome and steal
Gravities living cause our breaths comply with fleshly ash
Before we rise into high rise pitching handyman sails!
I won't worry don't you worry!
It's all smoothly killing me inside!
I'm drinking in places unknown tasting too much salt!
My lips forget what my eyes replay still depths are washed away!
Yelling to silent parts of me you'll never find a tiny life boat wading on time!
Secret sympathies orchestral maneuvers its dark it's so dark I gave you blindness!
Speaking in alphabets each day human praise did not arrive!
Escaping you escaping me laying down drinking butter wine!
Plastic clouds won't bring tears of joy!
You've got jump up to find equality of joy!
Continuous re wiring a head smoky tin!
Wild starry stained skies breech my absent words!
Goodbye!

Popcorn Skin

Popping scenic unequivocal scene of light
You stand below accents of street lamps proposing verses of rain
Curled inside a black thick coat telling me I walk upon breeze
Wild alligators swim upon roads hungry with impulsive
Don't cross main streets without a smile
Will you turn around again?
Popping in popping out
Sizzling inside your own heart
Lamented lines of angelic string
My cursive name etched in sounds of ambrose parades
Skin split questions?
You will walk these avenues again looking for paths of stone
Hidden stealing all stolen from your own immortality
Don't drag my shoes through sands of manifested waves
You will crash again
Into cement flowers lined in graveyard songs
Our human remains screams of tulip scented ash
Hungry tranquility slicing hourly bread a homeless ownership
We belong to no one
Ink paper style wet painted chairs in empty rooms prepared you
You pulled a rug from beneath your own feet
I don't want charmed ironed
Cells of men cells of blood locked granule veins
Our hemisphere a bubble of popcorn skin
Wrapped our eyes in silk bow boxes
Our distinctive insides bled by optical illusion
Generations of echoes repelling life's abyss
Sincerely optimal long fully accused

Translucent Lines

Noised feet shuffle over reflective pools of silence
Hue sits on a cusp of cities loud vanishings all will be gone soon
In your arms dawn is bare
Lines formed by translucency
Warmth's early gaze
Faces peel in frames of blames memoirs
Accents of liquid paint stretched across a night of canvases
Candle lined walls flicker in responding flashes
You blow out a wick to find days now absent
You seek sea outskirts for inward words
External possessions my poetic skin yields
Youthful expressions awaken with utopian notes
Don't clip my early wings I'm still alive
My words are spaciously burning upon infinite miles
A tiger's cage of rapid waves when oceanic quails fly
Shells of shattered glass I picked out of bled feet
My hands are protective breakage dipped in Gods childish ink
I play dead yet I live beneath my shadows voice
My mind skips corners of unrecognized soul
I keep time blissful of bodah!
Gull quelled flocks leave behind feral crumbs
Unremarkable fruitlessness squeezed with drumstick quotations
Lands of translucency roll over upon sandy lullabies
Effortlessly stealing cells of your bone
Don't break my tongue
I'm only walking back home

Sculptured Seas

Blue filled sunlight
Tides rise inside imaginative sails
Honey pollen shades painted by sceneries of silk movement
Oblivious only to myself lollipop stands wade above
Its candy hour seas scope of predictions
I create myself from lavas left by levitations
What's your rush I'm slicked out on sundaes dined apostles?
Trivially candescent I send myself into sculptured seas
Instantaneous interventions my life blood sweetens
My eyes are sounding heavy I'm tired of convictions
Designing principals out of evil pinnacles
My pots of clay spun with rainmakers
Sitting beside a swallowing swallow bird talking about dramatic peaks
I want to dive off a cliff headlong into effortless change
I could swear skies hunt me walking behind my echoic hypocrisy
I'm a shade on your porcelain stairs shiny radiant reflective
I cannot sing about you in ways I forget?
I don't want my own way I will go my own way!
Distantly distracted by planetary silence
Beneath naive opening hours of youth
Beneath weary noise of your perspiration
You spit water upon my face then say I'm blind
I want to clash in pale seas splashing out my name
Underground tornados will rise at my feet
I'm designed by hairs of wild rabbits
Acorns lonely falls stillness splinters of inks blood
Yet upon sculptured seas I turn around once more
Again with sincere forgetfulness of me

Petty Change

They call him petty words dribble from down his thighs
Boy bubbles drilled into walls upon avenues sweaty blows
You seized parallels of graffiti chained poems
Sprayed in sunken hollows above thick black lines
Outrageous rose tipped personification fragrantly fragmented
Petty words petty smiles petty change!
Zoo stained linguistics with mouths wide open
You cannot catch a wild bird
Don't pull threads from blue jean squabbles
I'll rip the pants off you!
Lay down here with endless soul!
Stop pulling skies from my eyes!
I'm hot with thoughts of airless jumps!
Trivial pursuits take a shot of my envious endeavors
I live for glazed sounds of lighter fluid ravages
Torn up with paper they wear lipstick livers
It's a fleshy world filled up spoonful s of youthful esteem
Don't touch cereal it's just grainy gravity
I want fruitful raisins dipped in life's honey lava
Breakfast lunch and dinner I'll eat words out of you!
My head is plied with colors of ink scratches
Malnutrition cannot exist without starvation
You'll never starve on backs of lettered worms
Ten legs long searching in vain
They say he's petty?
Remarkably versatile strung out by cruel ovations
Pinching your ears tunneling your skin
Bubble gum bubbles of poetic street fuel

Unemotional Reverse

They pour mud on your face then call it whipped cream
My tongues burning of tainted blood!
Implying unemotional rehearsal humans?
Strawberry boroughs cities of desensitized verse
Who's blowing whistles in my ear?
My hands are searching for soul inside skies of hot air balloons
Apartheid reversals colorless moaning
No one lives there?
Where's your unemotional confusion?
Inside whim less warriors words are faulty lines
Our living promiscuity stealing urchins out of wild seas
Salmon stained bears selling pizza
You keep taking gravy from children's eyes!
Your hourly assembles frozen with faces of chaotic fluency
Free sabotage expensive deaths!
Who has they're hands on you?
You cannot out of here in cell of disappear
We are poetically lining your pockets
God's enviable blood dripping with linguistic salvation
Humane slavery!
Worlds within worlds of dying soul!
Why chain this earth down when you want to go up!
Mosaic loveliness Rome's wolves!
We made fabric out of heroic conquers!
Sincerely unemotional sand riddled sculptures
Snake bitten lies!
Don't reverse over me too!
I've already written you out of my life!

Harsh Textiles

Flat surfaces I stand upon grounds of unapologetic reason
Glossy parades of sunlight stare back at me
Colored textiles burn away with hours of unspeakable meaning
Contributing in depths of sound
Lapsed sentimentalism ferments inside textile mosaics
Ink lines extracted by optimal distances
Juvenile clouds jumping in rhythms of poetic cinema
High wires pull your skin
Jack boxes jump looking for lions
Internal perspectives wade in roses
Kaleidoscope visions perpetuate your mind
Opulent waves of chance peaks within Gods eyes
Imaginative places allow a midnight's dreamy death
Scenic textiles seeds springing in air
Polystyrene windows shield plasticized sight
Empathetic propellers lift childish skies
Hungry dialogues created by stolen mouths
Poetically embraced voices search opulent streets
Enabled reflections infringe darkened houses
Candles held seen by a weightless heaven
Where's the other side?
Death will want you one day
Sailing into eternal fascinations
Blue silk seas
In harsh winds again you begin

Chemical Insanity

Chloroform telephones wasted ways ring in youthful ears
Collaborated murder sinister voices
Life line stroked swimmers why dive underground
Seas of illuminated water drowning in children's eyes
Pale faced insanity!
Rehabilitated laughter echoes into halls of empty chairs
Love died last summer our foolish chemicals now stained in glass
There are no prayers you gave your life away?
Aprils fools on wingless strings
You won't return again
Danced out rains of traceable unknowns
Streams of your silence bare dying seeds
Chastised liars!
Why did you fall upon broken glass?
Shattering pieces of your buried all beginnings
Young apprentices singing with collusions of insanity
Walk beside my surreal plastered dreams
I'll paint you with devastation
Unremarkable remakes!
Playful liars continue to call you away
Pay a toll take seat with Jesus!
You think you walk on water no one's there?
Horrifically imposing artificially bled
Wipe chain smokers off the map
You won't make money from honesty
Did you ever exist at all?
They still mix chemicals upon your headstone
While extracting stray bullets of gore
It's not about you at all!

Days Held

Nightingales skyward ink
We play in fields of anonymous eyes
Captivating hours sustained by beauty
Words are too simple for our eternal outlines
Bodies transfixed with poetic silence
Looking each for a breaking wave
Insatiable miles effervescently present
Immaculate intricacy woven in time
Man-made weather intoxicating voices
Minds reach over me populated by elegant stories
Gravity has prepared you for flight
Utopia lives in high spaces
Above opinion above denial you sing like a breeze
Youthful giggling Gods are turning night to day
Golden shades immersed in paint
Infinite belonging poetically motivated
Mortalities intoxicant splashes of enviable blue seas
Sensibilities nowhere

Faint Apparitions

Air tumbles inside sounds of yesterday
You've walk too hard
Grounds wishful compromise
Seasonal delusions
Apparent ghostly shades
Quietly manacled dialogue a minimal absolution
Configurations faint with praise streets of carelessness
Voices moving behind scenic exploration
Doorways leading into story tellers dreams
Lamented loves reveal trickling obscurity flat line
Photogenic cynics preaching liberty
It's all a game!
Don't walk into stop signs
Don't let your hair down
Wake up child
Granules of poetic silence will be heard
Bright blood a waits you on floors of charismatic doubts
Don't ever turn your back on me

Fatalistic High Dive

Words shallow in shadows blow you away
Sinister viruses bled noise
You've caught cold?
Emissary highs a ploy
Calculated cold senates empty chairs
Lonely loner's fatalistic birds
White water parades diving into skinless shrines
Did you touch seasons reminiscent of you?
Prowling fires speaking unknown dialogue
Thick black lines rehearse your name
Orchards of gravity fly over you
Endless hue I've seen you up there
In places where we missed ourselves
Gods stare at you through enviable darkness
Your head pinned to a world of confusion
It's not school there are no erasers to vanish mistakes
You live in your own poignancy breaking bone on air
Elasticized portraits dwell in homes off flowing abstracts
Don't paint sorrow on a wind chime
Don't sell yourself for gold
Opulent death
Making your own way to a table
Dive pool karaoke
Fatalistic mire
Keep your chin up
I smiled at you again
I stand in a place you'll never understand
Poetically modified effortlessly brutal
I wrote you into soul

Butler Charms

Tick tock sleeves
Pretty tipped egos
Keep wrapping daylight
Dawn's a warning
Just shuttering it's too early
Clusters dipped in airless paint
Weightless light
Serving escaping days
Cool air play headaches
Charmed geriatrics posing roses
Morbid telephonist bubbles
Conversations with quintet mars
Absolutions of accented skin
Strands of headless fire escapes
Empty windows of shattered glass
First day of April seized by satellites
My eyes are rapid buttons sunk in blue silk
Waves are pouring over sunlight
Minutes of ground hogs
Wade in silence
Inside it's snowing
Charms of gold
Immaculate indigo miles
I'm never out of place

Deux Fois Bleue

Marquee stereos
Thick stone pathways
Under water under my arms
My coat burns twice
Ghostly rain vanishes
Clouds are pure white
I won't walk here way again
Under water under my arms
Beyond myself floral rope
Silence inside you
Under water under my arms
Intrigues careless notice
Words infused by soul
 My infinite charcoal outline
Peacefully allured
My canvas of distant song
Under water under my arms
Weightless ink chants bleue
Twice sliced of me
Beyond love's translucent letters
My paper's thin skin

Fable

Buffalo tales rhino walls
Smoky thick picking yards
Quarantine words
Accessible excuses excessive burning
Absolute endings
Thick black strokes
Empty longevity swirling plays
I'm feeding sides of beef
Hungry wolves without hunger
Hours of designated knowing
Illustrious conversations with widows
Birds carve glass
Opulence a live white noise
Words are baking powder
Lightly toasted rumors you've told
Sweet flavors of soul
Find me in a song
My head's an arrow facing God
He's shown me open sorrows
Systemic paradises rundown
Empty houses with deadly men
Ascending resistant's
Cloudless waves raining
Senseless chapters threaded eyes
Mercy's chain
Sympathetic obedience
Prayer winged doorways
Sister fables of drunken coffee

Furious Peace

Love's silent rage
Infinite gazing passionate peace
Stencils' watch birds wade
Love slept in mortality
Who's counting time?
Café opulence
Jack's furious beans
My wild hare dialogue
Relays of starving praise
Waves of lively lions
Inhaling youth expelling myself
You spoke weightlessly of balloons
Cynically penned raptures
My underground heckling ink
In love inside my poetic virility
Outrageously contentious
Instantaneous with voice beyond daylight
I may find peace

Hive Street

Stung in amidst of blood wars
Graffiti pitched walls eventually vanish
You walk pathways of wet stone
Boats of catalysts remind you of storm filled winds
Captured in scenic pictures
Hive stung poems released into thin air
Wingless envelopes phrased with Gold ribbons
Street slang repeats of wounded shuffles
Stand behind my rope
Stop feeding castle cages
Crumbles of appetite radio
Leave behind static mercies
Collage capsules spin head strung words
Stand behind me
Rhetorical atmospheric questions
Play sounds of alligator wallows
You are sad
Bring me a thick black coat
I'm whistling at you

Infused

Blood clot cities
Pilot light gas
Explode!
Flick me scenic
Jumping skies
Infused predators
Don't say a word
Heavenly quiet find me now
Bounce your words off me
Plasticine Jesus!
Lollipop sweeteners
Speak in sandcastles?

Insatiable Dying

Strings of destructive taints
Lonely bare crossing across town
Charismatic cotton tainted curses
Insatiable bones
Let me sing?
Todays a great day for goodbyes
Shuffling shadows tender steps
Don't stand behind your old hats
Think of subway beginnings journeys underground
Place above place lined lands
Seeking windows with painted smiles
Spoon fed breaths
Childhood evaporations
Railway's deathly noise
I'll wind along easy paws
Optical sunsets replacing voices
Stretching yourself across avenues of immortality
Listening to ghosts
I see in between the vanishings
Beautiful moments to quickly they go running
Out of sight away from sounds
Insightful aero dancing under my skin
Exquisite chills performed in shadow
Loves fatal hearts declaring infancy
Chainless bodies appeasing wild essence
Life's born strangers acting new
Above dawn entwined by modesty
Souls infinitely wept by sands

Jumble Crumble

Scattered seeds
Hell left a hole
Streets of bottle thin lines
Jumble corn songs
Swing in jungles of Florence
Deadly silent crumbles
Jupiter's forgotten children
Rain felt eyelids
Heavy slumbers
I'm dreaming you away
Put a call into your widows
Canvas fitted policemen
Everyone's blue
Brick wall hysteria
Keep turning sideways
Grab a lift with shadows
Perpetual avenues lying to God
Never learning just churning waste
Garbage trucks filled with mindlessness
That's a tune of wild voice
Turn up the radio
I want desert!

Light Fluids

Effervescent fields ancient sparrow brigades
Cut my grass lift glass ceilings
Apricot fluidity waxed on ink
Lights tainted reverse colors
Carousel despondence
Tender tainted voice
Starry celestials turning backwards
Cloudy hangovers speaking fluent nosh
Prairies of burning ash
Left over love letters from Rome
I'm seizing your name on power lines
Electrical dismays ample cream
Cinematic flickering motions of sound
Picture frame memoirs
Stop breaking my nest

Yokeless Skin

Boiled soil underground aliens
Yokeless air ways
Crackling steam egg shell bell towers
Fly me away
Pulled under bridges
Streamlets of sinking skins
Stop kissing dirty water
Chemically peeled play doe
I'm building railways out
Over your head above your dreams
Rising industry omelet soaked hands
Stitched ink
Stop designing body bags
Nothing fits here
Tabloid head lines
News worthy ignorance
Pull my dice on yesterday
Take apart my spine
Finishing with alternatives
Cartoon paralysis out lined juice
Squeeze my bite
Let's run in pools of my blood
Splash me into divine saturations
I won't cry like a child

Aqua Stadium

Black and white outskirts paint me in ribbons
Silk collars drenched in black
I'm diving into depths of wet roses
Rainy seasons shiny seas
My skin turning blue
Pools of syrup soak universe
Appearances are deceiving
Don't blow out my candles
I'm breathing out sizable oxygen
Astounded by incisions did you cut me into repetitions
Adolescent configuration living inside your memory
Here now lost in tomorrow running on your insides
Aquatic collisions swimming backwards to find pictures enclosed
Shattering palaces of induction childish cartwheels
Keep spinning into terminology butterfly catching soul apprentice
Meet up high inside untethered clouds dreaming away eclipsed vision
Line after line poetically licensed swimming in stadiums above your head
Carousels of lilacs throwing petals to God
Alive in scented perfume staring straight into you
My echo a heart of children runs inside your eyes
I praise your lips gathering pieces of glass
Rhythmic paradise lost inside your blood
Move through my head beginning in my bones
Twisting turning effortlessly drowning
Castles of your eyes
Speaking in a voice heard by no one
Moments of us enlightened
Shaded heavens blissful seas
Swim inside me

Beautiful Desolation

Sway with me in arms of foliage
Hours lifted by falling just to see wild breeze touch your lips
Accents of winter perpetual chills
Isolated by promissory silence
Tilting lines with stains of ink
Need without want
Pinches of preconceived desolation
Nowhere is right here
Inside ourselves walking outward
Beautiful reaching strands
Humane flesh bone on bone rinsing walls
Walking into voices hearing shadows
Illusionary tales if I am right here where else could I be?
Eyes glazing over polished seas
Lying down in wasted sands
Even blood is spilt with beautiful resin
Pallets of bullet toned delusion
Justified objections excessive laid plans
Don't map your world with rice
Birds will steal your poetic propositions
Alienated by solid steal lively beauty
Quick step rehearsals just shout to me
I'll be standing still collected figures of imaginative frames
My lifelong jeopardy
Singing religiously amen
Sounding out angels dirty my hands in earthquakes
I'll rummage for causes building homes out of words
Prodigiously dignified happily desolated
Just an essence of words I leave behind

Caramel Fudge

Standing on a podium of heaven
Pulling strings from your hair
Sunsets of shaded skin dripping accented breezes
Splashing out words in water waist high
Creamy dreams effervescently descend
Licking engulfed souls
Your eyes appraised by scoops of weightlessness
Internal enclosures fixed stares
Piano playing astronauts
I dance in slippery seasons
Fudge trapeze winds carry me into airless ways
Seize my sighs run your hands over me
Quick strips of breathlessness
Pinning cinematic scenarios
Romanticisms of God
Will you reach this ground?
Flickering in petals of burning
Descending reflections praised by echoes of embers wild
Out there in the world your steps are aching shadow
If only to see again I will evolve in birds
In between scatterings of ash wings
Loves full blown eternity standing upon your stairs
My hearts captured essence
Searching everywhere without a place I already know
Café delinquents standing on chairs
Contemplating my voice
Carelessly triumphant inside you
I speak

Celestial Memoir

Sprinkling stars living whirling
Shine into me
Skinless planets
Gravities praise
Open my eyes
Could I run any faster?
Inhumane undergrounds emptied by sounds of you
Our careless voices seeking
Holding you in pause
Loveless loving
Opulent transparency
My legs sinking under seas
My sight evaporates with spatial glow
Currents of celestial mourning
Your presence in moments flickers inside pages
Books unread my memoir of falling skies
Born to die
Living without a sense of time
Glazier chills will follow you away
Breaking in senseless roses
Melted souls of burning sympathies
Impeccable seasons given by eternal praise
Paradise lost and found
My chance to die

Furnished Love

Our chairs are claws we have sunk into re-birth
Shiny floors release intimate reflections
I keep walking over to myself asking you
My hands hung like dangling windows
Can you see obviousness patting you back wards
Here in rooms of linguistics we are pale letters
I bite scratching days returning in smiles where did you lay?
Orchards stretched into seeds did you give away water
Maliciously returning my name?
Masculine air looms dusted with sand
Pulling apart blood strings
Staring into mild hours pleasing no one
We buy into material dreams of loves furnishings
Immaculate details of parental contusions
Copying breakages like shattered volunteers
Which way will you turn without a sale?
Combing nightly seas anticipating crashes
Silly youthful glory a heart in hand celebration
Entitlements of adversaries just smile I'll forget you
Don't turn your feet into bolts don't tie down luminous luxury
Liberal anatomies handing over biology's embryos
You love me not fainting eggs
Nest chain coliseums optional exposure
Stop reminiscing about empty rooms
You won't fill a heart of salacious mortality
Save petty pulmonary you'll have a heart attack
Don't furnish your life inside another person's disguise
Wasted high in love

Renaissances Diver

Taken apart by seas
My self-wading in depths 100% exploited
Searching for medium parallels
Skin tone diver resisting apparel confusion
Optimum equivalency wet parachutes with dangling shoes
I read into mirrors renaissances
Looking straight ahead evolving in my echo
I'd like to find my ego in diverse adversity
Weightless paperless poetically immersed
Strolling along lines of café conversions
Appealing myself with inherited eyes
Page less books won't hurt your head
Splendorous oppressive mercies
Walk in walking breeching your own birth
Tumbling into corners of solitary conceit
Wash down those words begin again make ink stainless
Glass house apprentices thin lip slurs
Our language constructed in halls of architects
Linguistic letters to specialists poems eaten on rye bread
Perpetual avenues never run out of distance
Stroke my shinning lead light
Heavenly minds heavy with verse
I won't build partitions from you
I'm a sleeping hierophant writing you into dreams

Sky Pockets

Your head enveloped by pockets of clouds
Whispering swirling drifting out of sight
Blue jeans worn in faded memoirs
Of a girl
Living high on breathing words
Angelic smiles passed into your hands
Slithering rolling tumbling beneath tall grass
Opulent speaking pulling out your tongue
Emptying yourself of petty change
You take springs water from of lonely eyes
Imaginative consolidation pushing one against the next
Ink stains your mind with embryotic fluid
Catching free seas in a midst of thunder
Standing under balcony of voices
Ghostly reminders paused in motion
Watching steps vanish in opposite directions
Questioning stillness
Days and nights impose articulated verse
Switching on street lights
Where will you go?
Turning out your pockets
Filling shelves with abnormality
Where's my cents?
Rose crested perfume alley way wilds
Extracted pieces of life's paper
Each ending a beginning
Songs of you discovered slowly dying
Insolated exterior tuning into God's radio
Sky faded blue carries me away

Solo

You singing on edge
Languishing breezes are eatable silence
Nature's charity cleansed with poetic voice
Walking into steps unknown sweeping up yourself
Fatally traced by crumbs crumbles
Sweet potato pie mash me in wine
Solo telephonic medium charms
When lights are gone I'll be home
Writing my way out
Drenched in apple chained perfume
A lined in conversable diversity
Solitary impede gaps you require
Noise of evaporation relinquished stories
I climb these lines pushing my head through clouds
Unsupervised with skeptics vision
Nobody's fool let harps accordingly play
I sing too alone with dynasties of motion
Wiring power lines with soul
Calling my own name?

Symphonic Notice

I left a note beside you
I watched you vanishing in questions
Keys of trembling played in shades of voice
I keep singing notice
My practiced hands replay a song
I keep forgetting to remember yesterday?
Incisory child's feet wading on my mind
Pinnacles of dance
I read waves of unknown seas
I write in absolutions of petty disregard
I am waking with you alive in mercy's belonging
I unlocking seeds forming my internal heaven
Words grow in unsalted industries
Solo heart symphonic bird I just keep beating
My flickering shifts with ghosts
Pulling sounds from pronounced clouds
Watery fluency ticks inside orchestrated fate
I shake my hair over page lined in ink
I haven't seen sun for weeks
Collaborating with myself against myself
My own champion
I cannot retrace where anyone thinks I should be
It's better a bird than a prayer?
Hung or torn down realities unimaginable
Just a girl
Obliviously symphonic
Systemically poetic arterially retained
My notice

Unknown Streets

Paused in slow motion a reminiscent smile
I turn around there's no one there
I thought I heard a voice
Lost in palaces of tuning gold
Shades of you return
You didn't understand breaks of rainy streets
Openly speaking opulently laughing
Youthful embraces held you inside captive windows
Openly you cried in silence
Serving away pieces of soul
Unknown to all but me
Sharing hours of priceless transfusions
Me to you returning into fragile skies
Brilliantly rising upon unspoken stars
Out fragrances of mortal burning
I sent letters to ashes
Signing my name across your soul
Bloodletting vigils eternity flashed in a second
No words could devise sentiment
We stood upon our own universe
Quietly embracing time
I live inside sounds of you
Paused enlightened lovingly sincere
Linguistic contusions verbally scented scenes
I held you there
I walked beside you effortlessly glowing
Unknown to all but me
Cologne fitted poems
Stereo fixed statics looking for space
Your voice plays a symphonic melody
No one else can see?

www.ingramcontent.com/pod-product-compliance
Lightning Source LLC
Chambersburg PA
CBHW060137050426
42448CB00010B/2171